THE GATHERERS

Indians of North America

THE GATHERERS

by Daniel Jacobson
illustrated by Richard Cuffari

Franklin Watts
New York/London/1977

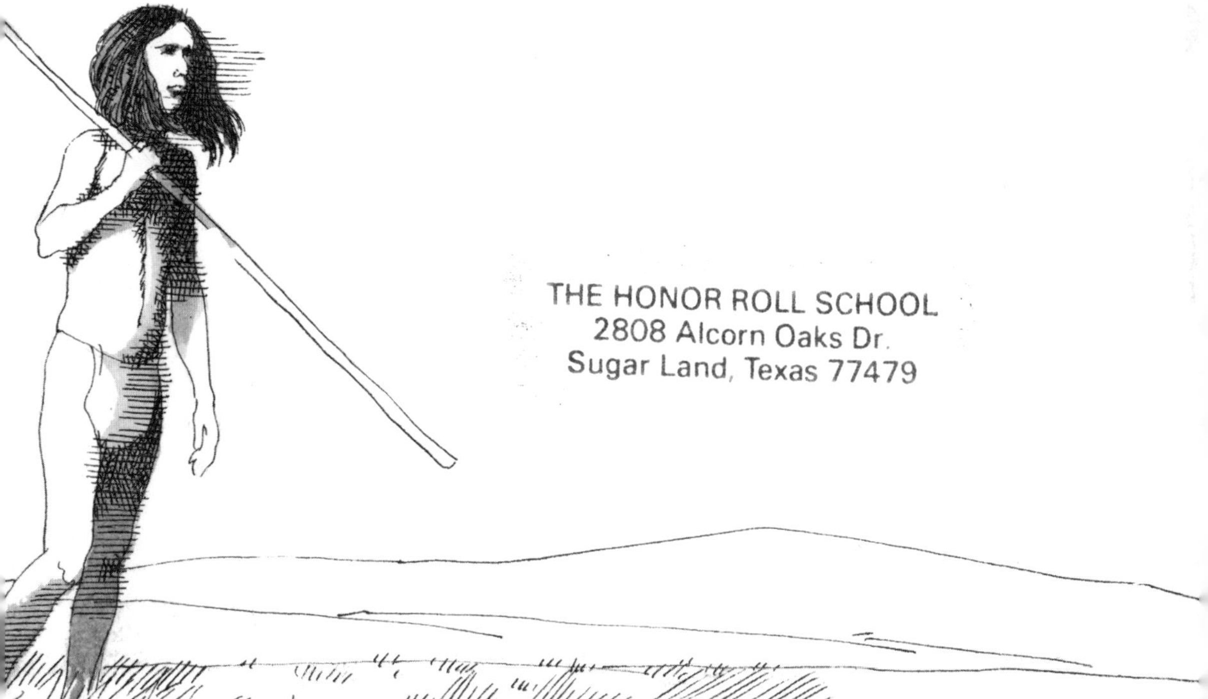

[redacted]

Library of Congress Cataloging in Publication Data

Jacobson, Daniel, 1923–
The gatherers.

(Indians of North America)
Bibliography: p.
Includes index.
SUMMARY: Describes the way of life, history, and customs of those Indians of North America known as the gatherers, with special emphasis on the Paiutes.

1. Paiute Indians – Juvenile literature. 2. Indians of North America – Juvenile literature. [1. Paiute Indians. 2. Indians of North America] I. Cuffari, Richard, 1925– II. Title.
E99.P2J32 970'.004'97 76-9810
ISBN 0-531-00326-4

Printed in the United States of America

6 5 4 3 2

>> CONTENTS <<

THE GATHERERS

>> INTRODUCTION <<

The Great Basin — 1820

From high on the mountain slope young Kwahadu (Antelope) looked down upon the temporary camp. Although it was early morning, the Paiute were already stirring. The men were carrying the long willow poles and water jugs, the women the skillfully woven burden baskets. The children, too, were up and about playing and running around the campsite. Kwahadu sensed what was about to happen. He knew it would be only a short time before whole families began to move upslope toward the pine nut groves.

Kwahadu did not budge. His eyes traveled westward over the familiar Carson Sink and northward to the Humboldt Range. He knew that the Kupadokado, the Ground Squirrel Eaters, had joined his own band, the Toedokado, or Tule Eaters, from beyond the mountains. A Kupa cousin told him that they had sipped water in the Carson Sink before moving on to the camp. The Kupa, as in past years, would take advantage of the pine nuts on Pine Nut Mountain.

When Kwahadu reached the pine nut grove the men were already at work, their long willow poles hooking or tapping the pine nut cones and sending them — along with the nuts and twigs — to earth. The men were not working alone. Many young boys were in the trees shaking the cones and young women below were packing them in their burden baskets. Tumplines in place, they carried the cones downslope and back to camp for cleaning and roasting.

In the heat of the autumn sun The Gatherers rested. They told stories, joked among themselves, and discussed the births and deaths of the previous year. They played games; they napped. Kwahadu even talked at length with Mua (Moon), a Kupa cousin, behind her brush shelter. Pine-nut gathering was a happy time for all!

The Gatherers could afford to be happy. Pine Nut Mountain had blessed them with a rich harvest. The Gatherers could look forward to a winter of plenty.

Gatherers All

The Paiute of Carson Sink were one of a number of widely scattered peoples in western America who spent much of their time gathering for their livelihood. There were gatherers in the Great Lakes area who gathered wild rice, berries, and bark. There were fishing peoples on the Columbia Plateau who gathered the camas root; the Coahuiltec of south Texas and neighboring Mexico gathered the bulbs of the agave, the fruit of the prickly pear, and the mesquite pod; the Pomo and other California tribes gathered roots, berries, and the all-important acorn. But The Gatherers – who most often scoured the hills for wild seeds and nuts – lived their lives in the harsh environment of the Great Basin, that vast area of mountain ranges and desertlike basins between the Rocky Mountains and the Sierra Nevadas. And this is their tale.

Many Questions

Who were The Gatherers? Where did they come from? How long ago did they arrive in the Great Basin? How did Kwahadu's people ever find Pine Nut Mountain? Did all of The Gatherers build brush shelters? Were there Paiute bands other than the Kupadokado and

Toedokado? Did all of The Gatherers climb the mountain slopes in search of the pine nut?

What did The Gatherers know of each other? What did they know of the world about them? What did they know of religion? Of birth, puberty, marriage, and death? Of curing the sick? Did they love and hate as we do? Did they fight among themselves or with their neighbors?

And very important indeed, are The Gatherers still with us? Have they in fact survived to the present day?

ASIA
Alaskan Land Bridge
Brooks Range
ALASKA
CANAD
Mackenzie River V
U. S.
MONTANA
OREGON
IDAHO
Great
WYOMING
Honey Lake
Pyramid Lake
Humboldt River
Danger Cave
Great Salt Lake
Lake Lahontan
Carson Sink
Lake Bonneville
Walker Lake
NEVADA
UTAH
CALIFORNIA
Basin
COLORADO
ARIZONA
NEW MEXICO

»1«

BEGINNINGS

The Gatherers were undoubtedly descendants of The Hunters who entered North America for the first time twenty to twenty-five thousand years ago. In pursuit of their food supply – the woolly mammoth, the old bison, the musk ox, and many smaller animals – The Hunters had trekked from east Asia far to the northeast. They had crossed the Alaskan Land Bridge, taking care to avoid the ever-present glacial ice. They moved north of the Brooks Range and came south by way of the ice-free Mackenzie River Valley. Over twelve thousand years ago *their* descendants were making animal kills on the American grassland.

But all of The Hunters did not remain on the Great Plains. There were those who moved eastward to hunt the mastodon in southwestern Michigan. There were those who crossed the northern Rockies into present-day Idaho to hunt the ground sloth, the old horse, the camelid, and giant jaguar – all now extinct – as well as the bighorn sheep, the pronghorn antelope, elk, deer, raccoon, and grizzly bear. There were those who crossed the southern Rockies into Arizona. Others also found their way – most likely from the Rocky Mountain areas or the Idaho hunting grounds – into the Great Basin.

Lake Bonneville
and Lake Lahontan

The Great Basin of twelve thousand years ago was quite extraordinary and far different from the Great Basin of today. It was much wetter then. The forests were more widespread and there were ample stretches of grass and a varied animal, bird, and fish life. So wet was the Great Basin, in fact, that the landscape was covered with a network of numerous lakes, large and small.

At least two were exceptional in size. Lake Bonneville, in the eastern part of the Great Basin, the forerunner of the Great Salt Lake, was over 300 miles long and over 140 miles wide. At times it stood more than 1,000 feet deep. Lake Lahontan, in the western part of the Great Basin, was somewhat smaller but covered nevertheless a great portion of northwestern Nevada and neighboring California. Honey Lake, Pyramid Lake, and Walker Lake are all present-day remnants of Lake Lahontan.

The migrating hunters, obviously attracted by the rich grass, the flourishing animal life, and the rare beauty of the many lakes, began to move in small numbers into the Great Basin.

Near the Edge of
Lake Bonneville –
10,000 B.C.

Kaska and his two young sons climbed to the top of the hill overlooking the lake. They could view the world from there in all directions. South of the hilltop the nearby swamp and beyond it the blue-green lake stretching for miles. North of the lake vast expanses of rolling grassland. And east and west as far as one could see, lush grassy plains and small lakes with a variety of animals – here a group of mammoths, there a small herd of old bison or a cluster of camelids – filling their stomachs with nourishing food or water. Kaska's eldest son noted a string of wild horses running at breakneck speed across the western grass. His youngest son pointed to the sky as an endless stream of waterfowl made merry above the waters of the lake. When Kaska turned to face the water once more, he was astonished to see before him the hulk of a giant ground sloth deeply mired in the nearby muck.

The Hunters, although taken by surprise, responded quickly. They scurried downslope to their small "camp" in the rock shelter. There amid the debris – wooden sticks and *atlatls* (spear-throwing devices that helped one hurl the spear farther and with greater power), stone knives and spear points – they found their favorite weapons: ten or more long spears.

Kaska pressed his left thumb into the spears' Folsom Fluted Points – the very same that had been used by his ancestors on the Great Plains. They were sharp and ready. Waving good-bye to his wife and daughter, who waved in return, Kaska and the boys started off toward the swamp.

The towering ground sloth – a male – stood silent in the muck. Only his front legs could be seen. His hind legs were sinking into the slime ever so slowly. The sloth tried hard to shake his body, to lift himself from the muck, but to no avail. A loud roar, which could be heard even at the rock shelter, split the air as the big animal continued to fight for life.

Despite the ground sloth's dilemma, Kaska and the boys approached the edge of the swamp with great care. They stayed on the high ground where possible. They tested their every step before moving forward. Closer and closer they moved.

Straining and tugging, the ground sloth made a great lunge forward. As he did so he was met by Kaska's spear, hurled with the aid of an atlatl, which broke the nodules in the sloth's skin and penetrated the very intestines. The sloth lunged once more, reeled, and was hit again with the boys' spears, once in the head directly above the eyes, and again in the front left leg just above the curved claws. The sloth's dying shrieks brought Kaska's wife and daughter on the run from the rock shelter as the sloth fell ingloriously into the muck.

The Hunters did not waste a minute. Knives in hand, they began to cut through the nodules. They ripped huge chunks from the carcass. Kaska's wife and daughter cut the chunks into smaller pieces. They all ate good portions of the meat raw.

They worked through the afternoon on the giant sloth's body. The boys and their sister carried the choice cuts upslope to the rock shelter. Shortly after their work was done, the saber-toothed tigers and then the dire wolves made their descent to the muck. They stripped the giant ground sloth to the bones.

The Changing Environment

In the centuries that followed, Kaska's descendants continued to live near the edge of Lake Bonneville. They made camp near Lake Lahontan and the smaller lakes. They continued to live their lives as The Hunters. But when the glaciers in the far north began to melt, the environment in the Great Basin began to change. The rain ceased to fall in abundance; the hot rays of the sun fell on the lakes and the surrounding countryside with brute force. The waters of the large lakes began to evaporate; the small lakes ceased to be altogether. The diminishing rain water could no longer support the rich forest growth or the lush grass. The trees on the lower slopes began to disappear; the grasses near the lakes and the neighboring valleys turned from rich green to pale yellow, and became short and tough. Then they, too, all but disappeared.

For the animals the environmental changes brought only chaos. The decline in water and grass spelled disaster for the mammoths, the old bison, and the wild horses. The camelids and ground sloths found it most difficult to obtain food, to find new watering places. Crippling diseases undoubtedly struck the big animals in their darkest hours. And The Hunters, compelled by the diminishing and uncertain food supply, made even greater efforts to make their kills.

The big animals were, perhaps, the first to perish, the first to become extinct. But neither could the saber-toothed tigers or dire wolves cope with the new environment of the Great Basin. They, too, became extinct.

It was time for The Hunters to make their decision.

The changing environment and the ongoing extinction of the animals had brought them face to face with the problems of their own survival. How would they cope with the new and changing world of the Great Basin?

Some, of course, would be unable to cope at all. They, like the mammoth and ground sloth, would perish. Others would attempt to leave the Great Basin to seek their fortunes in other climates and places. We have no record of their survival. But the majority would change their old ways, would make adjustments in their own lives to meet the new conditions. The Hunters in fact, in so doing, would ultimately become The Gatherers.

The Gatherers at Danger Cave — 7000 B.C.

By 7000 B.C. the major environmental changes had already taken place. Lakes Bonneville and Lahontan had all but disappeared; only the small remnant lakes remained. The lush grasslands, too, had virtually ceased to be. A desert vegetation dominated by sagebrush and shadscale clothed the gravelly valley floors. On the old lake beds – now encrusted with salt – only salt-tolerant plants could grow. The big animals, of course, no longer existed. And Kaska's descendants had long since abandoned their old weapons and ways.

Kochiba – one of Kaska's direct descendants many generations removed – and his band lived their lives near the salt flats on old Lake Bonneville. They were among the first of The Gatherers. Twenty men, women, and children made up Kochiba's small band. Their leader led them north from their late summer campsite on the Deep Creek Range along the edge of the Great Salt Lake Desert. It was early morning. The sun was only beginning to cast its rays on the eastern sides of the peaks that loomed high in the distance. But The Gatherers were already weary. They had been walking for hours. Their light burdens – the men and boys were carrying only spears and pieces of obsidian and chalcedony, the women and girls willow baskets and flat milling stones – seemed to be getting heavier. They stopped only rarely to rest. They walked on and on.

Shortly before noon the tired walkers spotted a spread of ducks and marsh hawks on the horizon. They knew they were getting close to their early autumn haunt – the small desert lake. They continued to move north. Then in the blinking of an eye the neighboring swamp and the lake itself suddenly appeared! The Gatherers dropped their gear, pushed through the bulrushes into the open water, and doused their heads. They bathed their bodies. They even drank the slightly salty water. The children played and frolicked about to their hearts' content.

In the heat of the afternoon sun, The Gatherers retired to the deep cave on the eastern side of the Desert Range. They chased the bats out of the inner grotto. Then, totally exhausted, they fell to the cave floor and went to sleep. They slept through the day and through most of the night.

Not until the following morning did the women – small stone knives and twined burden baskets in hand – leave the cave. They

walked slowly around the small desert lake and out to the nearby salt flats.

Kochiba's wife, Elka, led the party past the gray-green greasewood shrubs, the samphire, and the salt grass to a small group of pickleweed bushes. Few words were spoken. But the women and their daughters, who knew exactly what to do, went to work in earnest. The young women cut into the stems of the pickleweeds and severed them; the older women piled the whole plant – leafless branches and stems – into the burden baskets. The Gatherers worked all morning long, moving slowly from pickleweed bush to pickleweed bush.

They plucked the pickleweeds from the slightly moist ground and filled the baskets to their brims. Using tumplines, The Gatherers carried the full baskets back to the cave. On the cave floor the pickleweeds were permitted to dry.

For two full weeks The Gatherers toiled on the salt-white earth. They cut, gathered, transported, and deposited the pickleweed plants. Before long Elka noted that the tiny round seeds were ripe enough to drop from the branches and stems. She, her daughter, and others began to beat the plants against the edges of the baskets. Many of the seeds dropped off. But many did not. Elka, therefore, laid a flat winnowing tray on the ground, piled it high with the plants, and, holding the tray at both ends, began to toss the contents into the air. The wind, of course, helped her with her task. Before long the round seeds – now separated from the debris – were falling gracefully onto the winnowing tray.

Meanwhile the men and boys had been far from idle. In the confines of the cave they had fashioned from obsidian or chalcedony a series of small spear points. These were carefully made. They were quite unlike the old Folsom Fluted Point. They featured long narrow flake scars running across the face of the point and a median ridge that extended from point's tip nearly to the stem.

Spears in hand, Kochiba and the male band members trailed the antelope and the mountain sheep into the neighboring hills. Unfortunately they made no kills. Only later was their luck much better. On

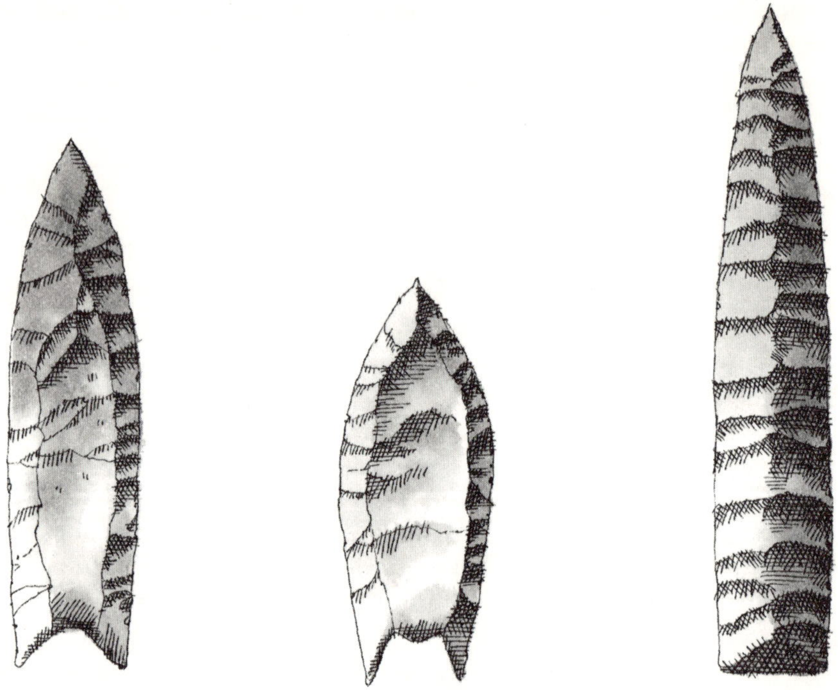

the desert floor they brought a dozen woodrats and jack rabbits to earth.

In the swamp near the lake (the men were helping the women) they gathered the leaves and stems of the desert bulrush. These the women chewed, thereby drawing off the plant's juices. They then expelled the pods of fibers from their mouths, the very same fibers that would be used in time to make cordage for ropes, bags, snares, and traps.

For the men and women both there were few idle hours, so difficult and time-consuming was the quest for food. But on one particular afternoon all of The Gatherers rested. They spread the chaff from the pickleweeds on the cave floor to prevent the dust from rising. They ate heartily of the pickleweed seeds; they washed the seeds down with the juice of the bulrush and the salty lake water. They talked about the distant past when their forefathers had first found the cave near the lake. They talked about the births and deaths of the previous year, about their long walks across the desert and up and down the mountain slopes. Kochiba talked about the beauty of the desert, about Elka and the day she had made her first winnowing tray from the willow.

But by late afternoon the women, their stone grinders in hand, were already pounding the pickleweed seeds on their flat milling stones. And on the following morning they were fanning out across the salt flats once more in search of the unplucked pickleweed bushes. The men, on the other hand, were already looking south toward the Deep Creek Range. Kochiba knew that his little band would soon be moving again.

»2«

A NEW AND DIFFERENT WORLD—1000 B.C.

For centuries The Gatherers trekked from water hole to water hole. They moved across the valley floors and up and down the mountainsides. They gathered seeds, nuts, and berries where available; they hunted the bighorn sheep, the deer and antelope, the coyote, muskrat, the jack rabbit. They continued to use the stone grinder and flat milling stone. They adopted the dart for use with the atlatl and ultimately exchanged both for the bow and arrow. They continued to twine their baskets but began to make new and stronger coiled varieties. They made rabbit nets, double-curved wooden clubs, and mountain sheep horn sickles. They continued to organize in small family bands, to live in the open or in rock shelters or caves. Kochiba's descendants, for example, continued to visit and even live in Danger Cave; they continued to gather the pickleweed on the salt flats.

But farther west, near the shores of a remnant of Lake Lahontan (it would later be called Humboldt Lake), a new and quite different world had opened for The Gatherers. It was attuned largely to water, to the life-giving resources of river and lake, to fish and waterfowl, and to tule and cattail; it was attuned, too, as of old, to the ever-important gathering of seeds, nuts, and whatever else the environment had to offer.

The Humboldt Sink

The remnant of Lake Lahontan tended to fluctuate in size. When the old Humboldt River carried much water the lake grew large; in flood time it even poured its waters into distant Carson Sink. When the river carried little water, as a result of high temperatures and high evaporation, however, the lake diminished sharply in size. Small pools of water then dotted the landscape. For miles the dense growth of tule and cattail was exposed. And beyond the tule and cattail – in times of low water or high – only the dry parched land, the sagebrush, salt grass, the tumbleweed, and near the mountain slopes the greasewood, rabbit brush, and rayless goldenrod. So dry was the Humboldt Sink area, in fact, that even on the surrounding mountains not a single tree would grow.

Nevertheless, the remnant of Lake Lahontan yielded numerous small fishes – varieties of suckers, lake chub, rifflefish, and black minnows. And to its waters were attracted thousands of geese, ducks, and pelicans. In times of flood, fresh-water mollusks were abundant. Numerous birds lived in the thickets on Humboldt River. The animal life, in the form of rabbits and ground squirrels, bighorn sheep, deer, and antelope, while not abundant, was certainly more than one could hope to find in the distant desert valleys.

And just over the mountains in the Stillwater Range was Pine Nut Mountain with its ample supply of pine nuts.

It was to these resources in the Humboldt Sink and neighboring areas that The Gatherers were obviously attracted.

Spring

Telaska knew it was spring. The new shoots of the cattail were beginning to appear above water; the red suckers were running in the river; and high above the lake the ducks and geese were flying, cavorting, and squawking. From the cave in the west face of the Humboldt Range, Telaska watched in wonder as three white pelicans started their dive into the lake in search of their prey.

And The Gatherers were busy. The women, tired of the dried pine nuts, fish, and waterfowl that had sustained them through the winter, waded naked into the lake in search of fresh "greens." They moved slowly toward the cattail shoots. Telaska's wife, Nelo, plucked a number of shoots from the muddy water and, using her thumbnail, stripped them of their brown soggy leaves. She then passed the clean white spears on to her children (they, too, were naked in the water) who eagerly pressed their lips into the new spring food. The Gatherers plucked and ate as the sun rose higher in the sky.

Meanwhile, the men and boys were also busy. They were interrupting the run of the red suckers with their dip nets. So thick was the run that Telaska's sons grew weary as they raised their long, beautifully twined red and chocolate-brown nets and pulled them – nearly brim full – to the river's edge. There they were met by the women, who only moments before had completed the cattail plucking. And they went to work once more.

Nelo, small stone knife in hand, cut off the suckers' heads, split them up the middle, and laid them on a nearby rock to dry. She slit the bodies of the fishes on both sides and cleaned out the entrails. She cut off the fins and carefully washed the remains in the river. She cut slashes across the fishes to keep them from curling, tied them together in pairs by the tails, and hung them on the nearby fish racks (a rack was simply a horizontal stick hung over two vertical ones) to dry.

While the men, women, and children were thus engaged, Telaska walked slowly into the cave. He dipped his hands into a well-stocked storage pit in the cave's floor.

He lifted a bag of rush matting from the pit and placed it conveniently near the pit opening; he did the same with three twined pack baskets and one large coiled basket. Beneath the baskets the pit was lined with grass, pieces of rush mats, and a myriad of basketry remnants. These were topped by two large stones. Telaska removed them all. Then he reached into the bottom of the pit and lifted from it a large package wrapped in rush matting. He emptied the contents: two rush bags full of feathers, three bundles of snares made of string and twigs, and eight remarkable duck decoys beautifully painted and feathered.

Joined by his sons, Telaska carried the buoyant duck decoys (two looked exactly like canvasback drakes) and three large double-nets down to the edge of the lake. They anchored the decoys among the tule stalks. The boys watched closely as Telaska ruffled the water with his fingertips, thereby imitating the sound of ducks feeding.

Before long a bevy of live ducks, attracted by the canvasback decoys, moved from the open water into the tule swath. From their hiding places in the tule The Gatherers swarmed over the approaching ducks, nets in hand. Taken by surprise, a number were soon enmeshed in the heavy twined strands. A precious few, more fortunate than the others, managed to fly straight upward to freedom.

That evening, in the quiet of the cave, The Gatherers discussed the day's toil, the failures, the pleasures. The men played a simple hand game and gambled until the sun set behind the distant mountain; the women attended to their children and repaired the nets damaged during the day. In the cool of the dark evening The Gatherers stretched themselves out on the cave floor and went quietly to sleep.

Summer, Autumn, and Winter

In late spring and summer the food quest continued. The Gatherers abandoned the cave. In family units they fanned out north and south along the western edge of the Humboldt Range. The women scoured the earth for roots; they gathered the leaves of the squaw cabbage; they journeyed across the floor of Humboldt Valley to gather the seeds of the tumbleweed. The men set up deadfalls hoping to catch ground squirrels, rats, or jack rabbits.

There was no respite. In midsummer the women and young girls went to the vicinity of the lake to collect the pollen spikes of the cattail; the men hunted the badger and coyote. When the wind rose in all its fury, sending blinding sand high into the air, The Gatherers, when possible, retired to the cave. They otherwise sought refuge in rock shelter or mountain cleft. Only when the wind subsided could they resume their toil.

In early autumn Telaska led his small band over the Humboldt Range to Carson Sink. There the band members rested, ate, and drank their fill of water. They walked slowly toward Pine Nut Mountain. Telaska pointed out how his great grandfather, many years before, had discovered the pine nut groves on Pine Nut Mountain while hunting the bighorn sheep. And many bands over the years had come to harvest the pine nut there.

In early winter The Gatherers returned to the cave. The women stored a portion of the pine nuts gathered on the mountain in the grass-lined pits. They collected the fibers from which fine cordage would later be made. They made tule mats, bird and animal skin blankets, and excellent baskets. Nor were the men idle. They hunted the rodents and broke the winter ice on the lake to spear fish. They made atlatls of greasewood, knives of flint and obsidian, pendants and scrapers of horn. They played games, gambled, and told stories far into the night. They watched the snow fall in Humboldt Valley. They waited impatiently for the coming of spring.

›› 3 ‹‹
THE NORTHERN PAIUTE

Telaska's descendants lived on in Humboldt Valley. Through the generations, their lives changed little from Telaska's own. They sought out cattail and tule, fished the river for plentiful sucker, and netted ducks, geese, and mudhens in the nearby lake. They searched the desert floor and neighboring mountainsides for seeds and berries. They journeyed to Pine Nut Mountain in years when the pine nut supply was ample. They hunted the deer and antelope with bow and arrow, drove jack rabbits into nets and clubbed them, and set deadfalls for small birds and ground squirrels. They continued to organize in small family bands.

In approximately A.D. 1000, small hunting and gathering groups, who spoke a Numic (Uto-Aztecan) tongue, began to push north from southern California. They filtered into the basin and range country of southern Nevada and Utah. They moved steadily northward. By 1200 or 1300 they had undoubtedly made contact with Telaska's descendants near Humboldt Lake. They visited with them, and perhaps even fought with them. We do not know. Stories told in recent times tell how the Numic speakers fought with the dwellers in the valley and how they threw fire into the cave in the Humboldt Range, thereby forcing the inhabitants to leave the area. But the stories may be myths. We do know, however, that many of the Numic speakers stayed on in Humboldt Valley, but not all of them.

Little bands continued to move in many directions. They occupied much of the Great Basin. By 1400 Numic speakers were already living in western Utah and southern Idaho; they had pushed north into northwestern Nevada and eastern Oregon. The eastern Numic speakers are known to us as the Shoshone; the western Numic speakers are called the Paiute. And the Northern Paiute are The Gatherers of history.

Northern Paiute

In 1820 the Northern Paiute lived in the Plateau–Great Basin–Sierra Nevada foothills area between the Blue Mountains in Oregon and Owens Valley and Lake in California. The heart of their territory, perhaps, was in northwestern Nevada – the arid valley floors and neighboring mountains, and the exotic rivers and lakes (remnants of Lake Lahontan) that dotted, and continue to dot, the Nevada landscape.

Small numbers of Northern Paiutes eked out their existence on the Black Rock and Smoke Creek deserts and in the upper Humboldt drainage. Their adapted life-style strongly resembled that of Kochiba and his small band on the Utah salt flats. Other and more numerous Northern Paiutes lived their lives near the precious water bodies of the Humboldt and Carson rivers and sinks, Truckee River, and Winnemucca and Pyramid lakes, Walker River, and Walker Lake. Their life-style was derived in large part from the traditions of Telaska.

Like the "old ones" the Northern Paiutes lived in families or family bands, named for the most part after one of their major foods. Thus the *Kamodokado*, or Rabbit Eaters, of the desert areas in the north; the *Kupadokado*, or Ground Squirrel Eaters, of Humboldt Sink; the *Toedokado*, or Tule Eaters, of Carson Sink; the *Kuyuidokado*, or Cuiui Eaters, of Pyramid and Winnemucca lakes; the *Agaidokado*, or Trout Eaters, of Walker Lake. Occasionally family bands

– such as the *Sawaktodo*, or Sagebrush Mountain Dwellers, of the upper Humboldt drainage – were named after prominent features on the landscape.

The family bands were strictly territorial. There were no band leaders as such; there was no formal band structure. A Jack Rabbit Eater, for example, who moved south to Pyramid Lake and made his home there would become a Cuiui Eater; a Tule Eater from Carson Sink who moved to Walker Lake would be known as a Trout Eater. If and when the newcomer returned to his or her old haunt, he or she would again be part of the old family band.

In the opening quarter of the nineteenth century, the Northern Paiute family bands ranged far and wide over the western Great Basin. Together with the Southern Paiute family bands, they numbered fewer than eight thousand.

Winter Village near the Humboldt Sink – 1820

The year had been a poor one for the Kupadokado. There was little water in Humboldt River, even less in Humboldt Lake. For miles around, the land lay parched and dry. Coyote, the trickster, longtime enemy of Wolf, the Good Brother, was obviously playing tricks on his people.

Sucker, chub, and minnow – in fewer numbers than usual – had carried The Gatherers through the late-blooming spring. Seeds, roots, berries, an occasional rabbit, and the ever-present ground squirrel had permitted survival during the long hot summer. But Coyote, in his own way, had not relented. In early autumn Mua's father, Kwina (Eagle), and brother had trekked to Carson Sink and beyond only to find that the pine nuts were very few on Pine Nut Mountain. It would scarcely be worthwhile for the Ground Squirrel Eaters to make the visit.

And to add to their woes, winter in all its fury was on its way. Temperatures were already dropping. In the mountains to the north the first flecks of snow had already been seen. It was clear to the Ground Squirrel Eaters that the year belonged to Coyote.

But Kwina, in his wisdom, did not despair. He had seen it all before. He had faith in Wolf. The first task, he knew, was to make certain that the Ground Squirrel Eaters were well prepared for a bitter winter. They must repair the *karnees*, or dwellings, damaged by the desert winds through the year and build two new ones to replace those that could not be salvaged.

From the tule near the lake Mua and her mother, Paxu (Sunflower), fashioned more than a dozen fine tule mats. They laid the willow pieces on the ground parallel to each other, covered them crosswise with tule strands, then topped the strands with other willow pieces. The willows (from top to bottom) were bound together with withes of sagebrush bark. Paxu examined each mat to make certain there were no holes showing. It would not be well for the winter wind to blow through the karnee!

Meanwhile, Kwina and his son, working nearby, had planted some twenty-odd willow sticks in a large circle. Around the sticks and only a foot or two from the ground they ran a length of willows, lashing them to the upright frame with willow withes. They did the same four feet from the ground, drawing the supporting willow sticks closer together. They repeated the process – in an ever-tightening circle – some six feet from the ground, thereby allowing for a smoke hole at the karnee's top.

When the frame was completed, Mua and Paxu, assisted by Kwina, carefully tied the tule mats to it. They worked from the bottom up, each succeeding mat layer overlapping the one below. They obviously did not cover the smoke hole. And they left room in the lowest tier for a door, which they faced east, or opposite the direction of the prevailing winds.

In the center of the karnee Kwina dug a circular fire pit two feet deep. Behind the dwelling a strong windbreak made of willows and brush was added. For the time being at least, Kwina's work was done. When his deep dark eyes passed over the winter settlement, he could

count six well-made karnees, a large sweat lodge, more than a dozen storage pits, and thirty-seven men, women, and children. How would they, the Ground Squirrel Easters, fare through the Great Basin winter? Whose year would it be? Coyote's? Or would it belong to Wolf?

Midwinter. By midwinter the neighboring mountains were covered with deep snow and the sink itself showed white in the low sun. In the winter village the storage pits were nearly empty. And the Ground Squirrel Eaters, wrapped in their rabbitskin blankets and eating little, huddled close to their fires.

Shortly after daybreak the men of the village, on snowshoes, and armed with bows and arrows, plodded north on the left bank of the Humboldt River. Kwina and son searched out the deadfalls they had set days before. They were empty. There was not a living thing to be seen – not an antelope, not a jack rabbit, not a ground squirrel. There was not a bird in the sky.

The Gatherers changed their direction and moved eastward away from the river. Just beyond a white-topped knoll they heard the howling of a passel of wolves. But the pack was beyond reach. They continued to move toward the mountain frame. Suddenly the rabbits! A pair, five, a dozen burrowing in the snow. The Gatherers pulled back on their bows and sent the arrows to their marks. Eight of the rabbits sputtered and fell. Just as suddenly the air was filled with a flock of birds. Again the arrows filled the sky; a half-dozen white-crowned sparrows fell quietly to earth. Late in the afternoon Kwina's arrows found their way into the flesh of four sage grouse. Kwina could well afford a smile. Wolf was having his day.

While the men were thus engaged, the women were hardly idle. For example, near the warm fire in her karnee Paxu was working with willow, making a burden basket. Nearby, Mua, also working with willow, was making a bottle-shaped water jug. By midafternoon she had completed it, having sealed it with clay and hot pitch.

In the other karnees there was similar activity as the women fashioned baskets, seed beaters, and winnowing trays. One woman was at work repairing an old set of snowshoes. And in the karnee

closest to the sweat lodge young Pagunupa (Cloud), Kwina's niece, was putting the final stitches in a rabbitskin blanket.

During the long cold evenings The Gatherers, exhausted from the day's toil, sat around their fires. They played a hand game, they gambled, they told stories far into the night. Paxu was particularly vocal. Originally a Cuiui Eater from the eastern shore of Pyramid Lake, she had moved to Humboldt Sink only after marriage and the birth of Mua. Consequently Kwina had lived at Pyramid Lake himself for nearly a year and he knew the area quite well. Paxu missed the lake and in the ebbing fire she often took the family back to her own childhood and her old haunts.

She liked to point out that Wolf, the Good Brother, had set the green-blue lake between the hills. That it, unlike Humboldt Lake, was ever full. That it brimmed with fish, ducks, and geese. She liked to talk about the island in the lake and the white pelicans that bred there. She spoke of the parent birds who stretched their wings over their featherless chicks to protect them from the scorching sun. She talked about cormorants, herons, terns, and sea gulls. She often repeated the tales spun for her long ago by her father. She liked to tell about the Cuiui Eaters who traveled to the mountains to trade with the Washoe. How they exchanged seashells and acorns – the Washoe themselves had traded for the items – for rabbitskin blankets and pine nuts. She liked to point out that Pyramid Lake belonged to Wolf. And when she spoke, the observant Mua noted tears welling up in her mother's eyes.

Spring Gathering and a New Life. Spring had come early. Melting snow from the northern hills and valleys had filled the slow-moving river with much water. Humboldt Lake, which had all but vanished the previous summer, stood shallow but wet in the desert. And The Gatherers, after the torturous winter, were glad to see Wolf return to the land.

The women moved quietly to the edge of the lake; the men to the river. Only Pagunupa, who was pregnant, and her grandmother remained in the winter village, for a birth was expected momentarily.

As in Nelo's day, the women waded into the lake in search of greens; they, too, plucked the cattail shoots from the shallow water. And they, too, passed the cleaned spears on to the children nearby. At the river the men were joined by seven young Tule Eaters and their wives and children from the desert west of Carson Sink. Every spring they came to seek sucker, chub, and minnow in the river.

The Tule Eaters dragged the water with open-twined baskets; they used spears tipped with the bone of the sandhill crane; they shot at the fish with bow and featherless arrows. But their luck was not particularly good. The fish were not running in great numbers. Kwina and the Ground Squirrel Eaters, on the other hand, turned to the hook and line. They attached their double-barbed bone fishhooks to the lines made of wild flax. They baited them with worms and grasshoppers. They waited patiently. But their luck on the first and second days was little better than that of the Tule Eaters.

Kwina turned to the lake. But before venturing upon it he must have a craft, a boat, perhaps two. He and his son, therefore, gathered four big bundles of tules and cattail leaves near the lake shore. They soaked the cattail leaves in the water, selected the strongest, and twisted the strands together to make rope. They tied a number of cattail ropes around each of the four tule bundles. Then two bundles were tied together to form the stern; the prow was made by turning the tule at the opposite end upward. After the stern and prow were both trimmed, a gunwale – also made of cattails – was added.

Two tule-cattail boats. One to carry the gear – spears, fish hooks, wild flax lines, and bait – the other for the fish if they were fortunate enough to catch them!

The cattail boats, which were exceedingly light and easy to maneuver, were pushed into the lake. Kwina and his son waded in behind them. They pushed the nine-footers toward the lake's center. Patiently they waited. Before long a school of suckers swam by, headed for the river. Kwina cast his spear again and again. So did his son. And Wolf smiled upon them. They made a number of hits and loaded their boat

twice. Paxu and Mua slit the fish up the middle, cleaned them, and hung them on racks to dry – in the tradition of Nelo set many centuries before.

Meanwhile, in the all-but-empty winter village, Pagunupa – assisted by her grandmother – had given birth to a baby girl. A new life – a new gatherer – for the Ground Squirrel Eaters.

The little girl was washed, wrapped in a rabbitskin blanket, and placed in an old basket matted down with sagebrush. While a number of the Ground Squirrel Eaters hovered over the newborn, it was grandmother who cared for her – and for Pagunupa as well. She even fashioned for her granddaughter her very first cradleboard.

For several weeks Pagunupa remained confined to the karnee. She nursed the newborn, watched her during sleep, ate very little, bathed, and rested. For five days Huna (Badger), her husband, also remained in or near the karnee. He did not touch a weapon, eat meat, or permit himself the joy of gambling during that period. He, like the baby's grandmother, attended in every way that he could to his wife's needs.

But summer was fast approaching. The desert seeds, the pollen of the cattail, and an assortment of berries were all ready for the gathering. The Gatherers fanned out across the desert. They carried their burden and winnowing baskets, their seed beaters, their water jugs, their blankets with them. They would sleep under the stars. The jubilant Pagunupa, eager to help, joined them. She carried her baby, swaddled securely in her cradleboard, in the comfort of her left arm.

Rice Grass, Deadfalls, and a Marriage. North of the winter village, yet near the river, the women moved into a favorite summer haunt – a wide swath of bunch or rice grass. Stone knives in hand, they cut down the tall blades of grass and carried them by the armload to a long flat rock near the riverbank. Paxu and Mua were particularly busy. They had built a small fire near the rock and were moistening with river water the grass shoots that contained the largest number of seeds. They threw a small number of shoots into the fire. The onlookers watched carefully as the fire consumed the grass but allowed the hard-shelled seeds to fall into the accumulating ash.

Paxu dropped the rice grass seeds into a winnowing tray and rid them of the surrounding debris. She removed the husks by rubbing the seeds on the flat rock and winnowing them in the open air. Before the end of the day she had ground the seeds between milling stones, producing a flour, and had prepared a tasty gruel, which The Gatherers thoroughly enjoyed.

The men, abandoning the river, moved east toward the mountains. They set simple deadfalls – stick, tilted stone, and bait – for crushing ground squirrels and woodchucks. They constructed more elaborate deadfalls, often weighted with many stones, for making wolf and wildcat kills. Kwina was fortunate enough to make several jack rabbit hits using arrows tipped with hard greasewood. He killed three magpies. But for the most part the hunting was poor. The disappointed and downhearted Ground Squirrel Eaters returned quite downcast to Humboldt Sink.

In late summer the Ground Squirrel Eaters were joined by a number of family bands from the north and south. The Sagebrush Mountain Dwellers had arrived in the sink area from the north; the Tule Eaters, Kwahadu among them, had arrived from Carson Sink. While the men fished in the river or set duck decoys (similar to those set by Telaska) in the lake, the women walked farther upstream. They moved into the buckberry groves where the lush red berries were ripe for the picking.

During the final day of buckberry gathering, Kwahadu's mother edged her way toward Paxu. Searching for words, she blurted out how difficult it had been to make the trip from Carson Sink, how it was hotter than usual, how glad she was to be in the shade of the trees along the Humboldt. Paxu listened but she, too, fidgeted for words. While she beat the buckberry branches with a stick, she talked about the visitors from the north, about the cuiui in Pyramid Lake, and finally in dead earnest – about Kwina's ability as a hunter.

Was Kwahadu as capable? Could he find the mark with bow and

arrow? Was he able to build deadfall and trap? Could he go for days without the benefit of a water jug? Would he be kind and considerate to the quiet raven-haired Mua?

By late afternoon the mothers of the potential mates had agreed that a marriage between Kwahadu and Mua would be a fortunate one indeed. The families had known each other for years. Kwahadu's mother – albeit at infrequent intervals – had watched Mua grow into womanhood. And Kwina had often remarked that it was Kwahadu that he would choose for his own son-in-law.

In the cool of a late August evening, Kwahadu slipped away from the family encampment and moved toward the open ground where Mua and her family were sleeping. Nearby he found a favorable spot and with Mua's image burning in his mind he went restlessly to sleep. On the two succeeding nights he moved closer and then closer to Kwina's encampment – closer to Mua. Early on the fourth evening he brought in a jack rabbit – a kill for his intended – and presented it to Mua. Mua accepted the offering. On the fifth night the delighted Kwahadu slept under the stars with Kwina's family. The raven-haired Ground Squirrel Eater was now his wife.

Pine Nuts and Circle Dance. In early autumn the Ground Squirrel Eaters trekked to Carson Sink and beyond. They joined Kwahadu's old family near Pine Nut Mountain. They built temporary dwellings of tree limbs and sagebrush and gathered pieces of wood for the evening fires. With the coming of the morning sun they prayed for their own good health and for the kindly smile of Wolf.

They played games. "Shinny," in which the men and women both participated, often on opposite sides, was a favorite. They gambled as of old. Who would score the most goals? Who would get hurt in the fracas? Which side would win? The old men – and, yes, the old women – gossiped and exchanged thrice-told tales. The children frolicked under the Great Basin sun.

One evening – in an all-night event – The Gatherers danced. They were assembled by Kwahadu's father, a fine singer whose voice,

Kwina suggested, could be heard far beyond the neighboring mountain. Around a tree they did the Pine Nut Dance – a circle dance that would help brings the rain and keep the pine nuts from shriveling on their branches.

Six men formed the original circle. They then recruited the others. But the women often selected partners. Paxu asked Kwina to dance; Mua called upon Kwahadu to join the ever-widening circle. Before long some fifty men and women, moving shoulder-close, were shuffling clockwise around the tree. Kwahadu's father urged the dancers to join him in his song. The singing filled the valley.

Shortly before midnight old Tsaivu (Tule), Kwahadu's grandmother, water basket in one hand and sagebrush twig in the other, began to dance her way around the circle in a counter-clockwise direction. She dipped the twig into the water and doused the ground. It was The Gatherers' way of asking for a harvest of many pine nuts. She then tossed a number of pine nuts liberally over the ground – the symbol for returning to the earth what you were taking from it, long a Paiute custom.

The dancers danced the whole night through. They rested through most of the next day. Then there was more merriment and finally the assault on Pine Nut Mountain.

In the tradition of Telaska, The Gatherers beat the pine nuts from the trees and collected them from the ground. They moved steadily upslope. They filled their burden baskets. Wolf; the Good Brother, had smiled upon his people once more.

The Gatherers had eaten their share; they had also stored their share. By midautumn the Ground Squirrel Eaters, Kwina and Paxu, were making the long trek back to Humboldt Sink.

Communal Rabbit Hunt. Late in the autumn the Tule Eaters and the Sagebrush Mountain Dwellers returned once again to Humboldt Sink. They made merry as always. At the same time they were very serious. For how long would the pine nuts, only recently gathered, last? Would the supply in the storage pits get them through the winter?

How would the cold season go for the Sagebrush Mountain Dwellers who, living in the extremely arid north, had no access to the life-giving pine nut at all? They, in particular, had ventured to Humboldt Sink in the hope of procuring the meat of the rabbit.

Kwina organized the rabbit hunt. The Ground Squirrel Eaters were sent to the river with their nets. They strung them out, using low bushes to anchor them, in a wide semi-circle between a low knoll and the river itself. All the Tule Eaters and Sagebrush Mountain Dwellers, including women and children, beat the bushes for the rabbits. Then they came together. In a human screen they moved toward the river forcing the rabbits into less and less space.

The rabbits would not move into the river. They were forced to follow the streambed north. The Gatherers followed them. And the rabbits, seeking freedom, rushed pell-mell into the low-strung nets. They became entangled in them. And the Ground Squirrel Eaters, waiting eagerly behind the nets, clubbed them to death.

The Tule Eaters stayed in Humboldt Sink for nearly three weeks, the Sagebrush Mountain Dwellers for over a month. The men skinned the rabbits and cut the pelts into ribbons; the women saw to it that portions of the meat were dried. And while the Ground Squirrel Eaters stored their share of the dried meat in the pits at the winter village, the women of the visiting family bands put their share in burden baskets and prepared them for the long trip home.

The visitors left Humboldt Sink well before the coming of the first snow. But the days were getting colder. The frost was already on the sagebrush. For the Ground Squirrel Eaters the winter villages were beckoning.

Sickness and Death. In Humboldt Sink the winter winds began to howl, the snow to fly. The valley was soon engulfed in white. Visibility grew worse with the hours, and walking – even with the aid of snowshoes – was difficult, if not impossible.

The Ground Squirrel Eaters tended their fires. They tried desperately to make merry. Instead, however, a general sadness, a deep

gloom, settled over the winter village. Pagunupa, mother of her yet unnamed baby, lay ill in the karnee near the sweat lodge. She appeared to be near death. She breathed heavily. Her hands searched for her abdomen. She clenched her fists.

Tazinupa (Star), Kwina's uncle and a long-time shaman whose powers had come to him in a dream many years before, hovered over the body. He began to sing. He waved the pelican's beak in his right hand over Pagunupa's abdomen. Others joined in the singing as Tazinupa went into a trance. His own body stiffened. But he soon came out of it. When Tazinupa moved his arm to the right, Pagunupa moved hers in the same direction. When Tazinupa shuddered, Pagunupa shuddered in turn.

The shaman continued to sing. He pressed his lips into Pagunupa's abdomen as if to suck the pain from her body. He passed two eagle feathers over the abdomen. He uttered many words.

In the weeks that followed Pagunupa rested. She grew stronger. She ate boiled roots and flowers – the cliffrose among them – and sipped a tea made from the sage over which Tazinupa passed his hands. And before long Pagunupa was up and about, nursing her baby and making a new water jug from the willow. Tazinupa – with the assistance, perhaps, of Wolf – had helped to save a Paiute life.

But there was no help he could offer Pagunupa's mother, the unnamed baby's grandmother. She passed away in the middle of a cold Great Basin night. Her body, tied with arms and legs flexed and wrapped in a rabbitskin blanket, was carried through the snow to a crevice in the neighboring mountainside. There she was laid to rest.

On the very same day the Ground Squirrel Eaters burned the dead woman's karnee. They did not want the spirit of the dead to return to the village. And out of fear for the dead they would never again utter her name.

Pagunupa and her family moved into the sweat lodge for the remainder of the winter. They went into mourning. They ate little meat and did not bathe. They streaked their faces with earth. They cut their hair.

And the snow continued to fall in Humboldt Valley.

4

EUROPEANS AND AMERICANS

The Gatherers had adjusted well to the environment of the Great Basin. They had roamed for centuries over its wide expanses. They had created – through borrowing and their own mettle and initiative – a way of life in which they could take pride, in which they could feel secure.

But they had few illusions. They were keenly aware that life was a struggle, often a bitter one, between Coyote, the trickster, and Wolf, the Good Brother. Coyote, using his wiles, often duped his people, often brought them painful moments, even catastrophe. Wolf, on the other hand, did everything possible to bring The Gatherers joy and contentment. The struggle appeared to be one among equals.

And then there were the bearded strangers!

Europeans! Americans!

They would enter The Gatherers' world from the south, the north, and finally from the east and west. They would bring with them new and different ways of life, new and different ways of looking at the world.

Who were the newcomers? Where were they coming from? How would The Gatherers react to them? How would they cope with their numbers, their new and different ways? What would happen to Kwina and Paxu? to Kwahuda and Mua? to Huna and Pagunupa? to the Ground Squirrel Eaters? the Tule Eaters? And, yes, how would Coyote, the trickster, and Wolf, the Good Brother, react to the strange bearded faces? And what would happen to *them?*

The Europeans

The Spaniards had been the first of the Europeans to enter the arid interior. Father Francisco Garces had crossed the Colorado River and entered the Great Basin on March 7, 1776. Fathers Francisco Dominguez and Francisco Escalante, exploring the possibilities of an overland route between Santa Fe and Monterrey, had crossed the Colorado farther north in autumn of the same year. They had forded the Green River (they called it the San Buenaventura) and crossed the Wasatch Mountains into the Great Basin. They later moved on to Utah Lake and journeyed south along the banks of the Sevier River.

The good fathers thought that the Green and Sevier were one and the same streams. And the cartographer, or mapmaker, of the expedition put them on his map as such. Later, other cartographers followed his example. They even extended the so-called San Buenaventura much farther west. The idea that it dropped its water into The Great Sea (Pacific Ocean) – just as the Columbia River did – became quite popular. Other explorers and adventurers would search the Great Basin in an effort to find the mysterious river.

The English, eager to find new trapping grounds in the vast interior, moved into the Great Basin from the north. From Fort Nez Percé the first of the so-called Snake River Expeditions moved into the Bear River area (1818) north of Great Salt Lake. The fifth Snake Country Expedition (1828–1829), led by Peter Skene Ogden of the Hudson's Bay Company, struck the upper Humboldt River on November 9, 1828. Ogden simply called the river the "Unknown River," for he knew so little about it. In a parley with the Sagebrush Mountain Dwellers he learned that the river went south and entered a large lake. The "Unknown River" was certainly not the San Buenaventura!

Ogden Meets the Ground Squirrel Eaters. The following spring Ogden's party moved south along the "Unknown River" once more. On May 30, 1829, the Ground Squirrel Eaters (some armed with bows and arrows) greeted them from the tule swath just east of Humboldt Lake.

Kwina had been aware of Ogden's movements for days. For safety's sake he had sent Paxu and the other women and children to the neighboring mountains. They were joined there by other families of Ground Squirrel Eaters. Kwina and a number of other men, meanwhile, lay concealed in the tule. They would watch, wait, and surprise the bearded ones!

Joined by a small contingent from the hills, the Ground Squirrel Eaters walked to within five hundred yards of Ogden's temporary camp. They waited.

But not for long! For Ogden himself approached them on foot. He held out a pouch of tobacco for Kwina. The Ground Squirrel Eater hesitated for only a moment, then took the tobacco pouch in hand. He smiled and bid the much-relieved Ogden welcome to Humboldt Sink!

Ogden remained in the territory of the Ground Squirrel Eaters for six days. He was under Kwina's constant surveillance.

During the day the inquisitive Ogden asked many questions. And Kwina answered those that he wanted to answer. What is beyond the lake to the west and south? Is there another water body nearby? If so, how long will it take to get there?

Kwina pointed out that there was a vast desert to the west, that it would take many days to travel to the western river (the Truckee) or the western lake (Pyramid Lake). The journey was a difficult one.

On the sixth day the trappers broke camp and moved north. Kwahadu and Huna trailed them upriver.

It was late November before Ogden returned to Humboldt Sink. By that time the water bodies were choked with ice and snow. The Ground Squirrel Eaters were nowhere to be seen. They were guarding their fires a few miles away in their winter village.

Ogden stayed for two days. He then turned southward to Carson Sink and across the desert to Walker Lake and beyond.

An Appraisal of the European Impact. The Spaniards had made the first *entrada* into the Great Basin. But they had not contacted The Gatherers at all. The English trappers had moved into the Humboldt drainage. They had come into contact with the Sagebrush Mountain Dwellers in the north, with the Ground Squirrel Eaters at Humboldt Sink, with the Trout Eaters at Walker Lake. But their impact on the world of The Gatherers was very slight. It was left for the Americans to bring the onslaught.

The Americans

The American fur trappers and traders, checked by the Blackfeet and Arikaras on the upper Missouri, began to shift their operations farther west and south. Jedidiah Smith, a Rocky Mountain Fur Company employee, crossed the Rockies via South Pass in 1824. In July of the following year the first real rendezvous between the trappers, or mountain men as they were called, and their suppliers from the east was held on Henry's Fork. By 1826 the mountain men had moved even farther south. They had become quite familiar with the country near Great Salt Lake. They could hold their rendezvous in Cache Valley within the Great Basin itself.

Jedidiah Smith, who was interested in trapping the beaver, selling the fur in California – some say in China – and, perhaps, in locating the San Buenaventura, left Cache Valley soon after the rendezvous. He proceeded south by way of the Virgin and Colorado rivers, west over the trail earlier blazed by Garces to the San Gabriel Mission in California, and, after difficulties with the Mexican governor of California, north by way of the San Joaquin River.

Smith then crossed the Sierra Nevada Mountains, passed through the area south of Walker Lake, which was best known to the *Pakwidokado*, or Chub Eaters, and continued across the central part of the

Great Basin. He arrived at Great Salt Lake in early July, 1827, and journeyed north to Bear Lake for the summer rendezvous.

Jedidiah Smith had opened up much of the Great Basin for future American activity. Unfortunately, however, he had found few beaver streams. He had certainly not found the San Buenaventura and, moving across the central portion of the arid interior, he had missed entirely the Ground Squirrel Eaters of Humboldt Sink.

Joseph Walker and the Encounter at the Sink. Six years later, however, Joseph Walker would meet the Ground Squirrel Eaters. The young mountain man, whose motives for exploring were similar to Smith's, moved west across the salt flats from Great Salt Lake. His party struck Ogden's River and followed its banks west and south. Young Sagebrush Mountain Dwellers, shy but curious, harassed the party constantly. In the dead of evening – as if in fun – they would make off with the traps, pick up items of clothing, send the horses scurrying away from the bearded ones' camp.

One day, in a fit of rage because an Indian had taken one of his traps, one of Walker's men fired upon two innocent Sagebrush Mountain Dwellers fishing on the riverbank. He killed one and in a frenzy threw him into the river. The other escaped to the nearby hills to tell the lurid tale.

The harassment continued. It increased as The Gatherers came together from the outlying hills and valleys and followed Walker's party downstream. And word of the tragedy, passed swiftly along the river, reached Kwina and the Ground Squirrel Eaters just before their intended journey to Pine Nut Mountain.

Near Humboldt Sink, Walker set up his temporary camp. According to reports, several hundred Gatherers approached the campsite with caution. Some two hundred yards from the bearded ones they all sat down.

Kwina, Kwahadu, Huna, and two middle-aged men from the neighboring family bands rose and moved toward the Walker campsite. They offered to smoke with the bearded ones. But Walker, hesitant and fearing the worst, refused. He pointed out that he would be willing to talk to the Indians halfway between the campsite and where the Indians were sitting. Kwina refused!

Meanwhile, The Gatherers, growing fidgety, began to move in the direction of the river. Walker's men raised their guns but did not fire. They warned The Gatherers to keep their distance or they would certainly be killed. The Gatherers disappeared into the black evening.

On the following morning Walker's party began to move into the sink itself. The Gatherers nearly surrounded them in the tule swath. It was as if they were playing a game. They made no move to hurt Walker or any of his men in any way.

The bearded ones were free to go. They began to move west onto the desert. The young men among The Gatherers followed them and continued to harass them against Kwina's advice. Kwina and the others pursued the young Gatherers. They urged them to return to the sink. But they would not listen.

Harassed, much worried, fearful, and spurred on by the hotheads in his party, Walker finally gave the order to fight. Thirty-two of his men quickly mounted their horses and just as quickly surrounded the young men in the Indian group.

They opened fire and perhaps as many as thirty of The Gatherers – the very finest of their young men – perished in the onslaught. Coyote had played another trick – this time on the flower of his people.

The Ground Squirrel Eaters – certainly not the only losers – had lost many young men. Kwina, in the sweat lodge at the winter village, stared in disbelief at the rabbitskin blanket beneath him. He wept.

He and the Ground Squirrel Eaters would never forget the encounter at Humboldt Sink.

The California Trail. After the battle Walker moved west and crossed the Sierras into California. He wintered there. In the spring he returned to the arid interior by way of Walker River. And after another battle with the Ground Squirrel Eaters he moved north and east along the Humboldt.

As a result of his travels (and in spite of the bloodshed), Walker had helped to define for Americans a portion of a major route west. It would in time be called the California Trail.

From near Fort Hall travelers were urged to go south by way of Raft River, to Goose Creek and Thousand Springs Creek and on to the Humboldt – the artery that made the trail possible – then south to the sink. There the western travelers could cut the grass for their animals and store precious water in their containers for the forty-mile haul across the desert. After which they could move up the Truckee, through its canyon – or turn up the Carson Valley – and over the Sierra passes into California.

A small party of adventurers began to trek west over what was to become a portion of the California Trail in 1841. In 1843 another party, with Joseph Walker as its guide, went south by way of the Humboldt, but approached the Sierras from Walker River. It was left for the Elisha Stevens party of 1844 (forty-six people and eleven wagons) to etch, with the marks of its wagon wheels, the California Trail.

In succeeding years the number of wagons using the trail increased considerably: fifty wagons in 1845, several hundred in 1846. And then, with the discovery of gold near Sutter's mill in California in 1848, there was a mass movement of people, wagons, and animals. Over 21,000 people, more than 6,000 wagons, between 40,000 and 60,000 mules, oxen, and horses, traveled the California Trail in 1849!

For Kwina and the Ground Squirrel Eaters, who watched from the nearby mountains, the never-ending movement of the white-topped wagons was shattering. Kwina watched as the yoked oxen lumbered along past the swath of rice grass, past the lush buckberry groves aflame in color. He watched as they chewed on the native grasses and drank their fill of the Humboldt's water. Kwina watched the Americans fish and bathe. He watched them hunt the antelope and rabbit.

The Gatherers, half-starved and filled with anguish, could do little more than watch. It was impossible for them because of the great number of Americans and arms to get to the river or lake to fish or set their duck decoys in place. It was impossible for the women – Paxu, Mua, Pagunupa – to gather the rice grass or the buckberries. And when The Gatherers fanned out across the bleak desert they found it next to impossible even to bring in the jack rabbit – so effectively had the Americans ravaged the countryside.

The Ground Squirrels were utterly confused. But they did not panic. They talked. They counseled.

Kwahadu would fight. He would drive the Americans out of the sink, out of the valley, out of the desert. Huna would raid the wagon trains for food. He would kill the enemy only if necessary. Others thought it best to leave the sink. They would join the Tule Eaters in the desert. Kwina, urged on by Paxu, made it known that he wanted to journey west to Pyramid Lake, to the land of Wolf.

Pyramid Lake. Captain John C. Fremont, on his expedition south from Oregon (1843–1844), "discovered" a lake, ". . . a sheet of green water . . ." in the mountains of western Nevada. He called it Pyramid Lake after the large rock near the eastern shore that he thought resembled the great Egyption pyramid of Cheops.

Just south of the lake, on the Truckee River, Fremont found a winter village of the Cuiui Eaters. There he and his men were treated to boiled, fried, and roasted cutthroat trout. It was a feast the captain and his aides would write about and long remember.

The Cuiui Eaters netted and speared the cuiui near the mouth of the Truckee in early spring; they gathered mustard and mentzelia seeds and the red berry of the desert thorn. In summer they labored in the rice grass, in the buckberry groves. They moved to the neighboring hills for the pine nut in autumn and caught the jack rabbit in the communal drive. During the winter months they fished the river for the cutthroat trout. They lived their lives much like the Ground Squirrel Eaters of Humboldt Sink.

For Kwina, Paxu, their children, and grandchildren, who had made the move to Pyramid Lake, few changes in life-style would be necessary. The Ground Squirrel Eaters would simply become Cuiui Eaters!

Settlers, Miners, and the Pyramid Lake Wars. Changes, however, were in the offing. Soon after Kwina's arrival American settlers began to set up temporary stores and living quarters along the California Trail. John Reese built the first permanent trading post at Mormon Station in the Carson Valley (1851). And other Mormons followed.

After the discovery of gold at Gold Canyon (1850), hopeful miners appeared in the eastern Sierra hills. Franktown was flourishing in 1853, Johntown in 1856. Chinese laborers, brought in from California to build a water ditch between Carson River and the mines, were already living in "Chinatown" – the future Dayton.

In 1857 gold was discovered in Six Mile Canyon. In 1858 Carson City was laid out. And American numbers began to grow even more with the discovery of the great Comstock Silver Lode and the building of Virginia City in 1859.

The Washoe neighbors of the Cuiui Eaters – and the Cuiui Eaters themselves – were overwhelmed. The settlers and miners were pouring over their hillsides. They were eating their food, cutting down their pine trees, molesting their women. Herds of sheep, hogs, and cattle were devouring their grass. There were occasional brawls, killings.

Young Indian renegades – they were probably not Cuiui Eaters – retaliated. Several white men were killed. On May 7, 1860, Williams' Station, a whiskey shop on Carson River, was burned and its proprietors put to death. The white communities panicked. They raised a rabble of 105 volunteers at Virginia City under Major William Ormsby and set out to punish the killers.

Williams' Station was deserted. The rabble turned on Pyramid Lake.

The Gatherers were ready. On May 12, 1860, Old Winnemucca and Numaga (members of the Cuiui Eaters who had earlier spoken for peace) led the rabble into a carefully planned ambush. They nearly crushed them in a withering crossfire. When the attackers attempted to make a stand in a clump of cottonwoods near the Truckee they were greeted by deadly arrows and gunfire. The survivors retreated. They left saddles, guns, knives, and pistols strewn over the countryside. Major Ormsby and seventy-five volunteers were killed. A number of others were badly wounded.

The Gatherers had won the first battle of Pyramid Lake.

But the settlers and miners were not to be denied. On May 24, 1860, Colonel John Hays led 547 volunteers and 207 regular United States Army troops north from Virginia City to Pyramid Lake. The Gatherers – perhaps 300 strong – barred the way. They fought savagely (160 Paiutes were killed and as many wounded) in a delaying action as the main body moved north along the western side of Lake Winnemucca to safety and freedom.

Days of Agony and Change. The Gatherers had managed to survive. But their days of agony were to continue. Slowly the Cuiui Eaters returned to Pyramid Lake to the uncertainties of living on a reservation (not officially proclaimed until 1874); to the coming of additional squatters or "entrymen" to the lands; to the vagaries of the farming they were expected to engage in.

Telaska's cultural descendants handling farm implements, planting gardens! Tending cows and sheep! Driving teams of oxen! Wearing white man's clothing! The world was changing indeed. Coyote was in his glory.

And the rate of change was accelerating. Kwina and Paxu could hardly believe their eyes. South of Pyramid Lake there was much activity. Chinese laborers – and a number of Cuiui Eaters too – were grading the right-of-way for the new "iron horse." Track was being laid from the mountains, along the Truckee, and out onto the desert. On July 1, 1868, the aging Kwina watched diligently as a white man set the stakes into the ground where the town of Wadsworth would soon rise. Twenty-one days later the train itself would come rumbling over the track from the new site at Reno.

Workmen simply swarmed over the rails. By August 21, the track had been laid as far as Browns – past the Humboldt Sink; the rails were reaching up the Humboldt River itself. The Central Pacific Railroad would unite with the Union Pacific at Promontory, Utah, on May 10, 1869.

The railroad tugged at the Cuiui Eaters. With farming poor and prospects worse, with entrymen working their lands and their traditional foods in short supply, the Cuiui Eaters were pulled toward the railroad – toward Wadsworth – as if by a magnet. There they would go to work for the white man.

Kwina's son, for example, chopped wood and did heavy house cleaning for Mr. Abraham Newberry. Others worked as laborers on the railroad or on nearby farms. Kwina's daughter-in-law became a house servant; she did the laundry for a young couple in the center of town. Before long she would be called Sarah Newberry, taking her name from the family for whom her husband worked. She learned to speak English fluently.

The railroad served The Gatherers in still another way. Through an agreement with the officials they were permitted to ride atop the box cars free. Kwina could return to visit the Ground Squirrel Eaters and the haunts of his childhood – by rail!

The Ghost Dance. Farther south the Trout Eaters were also having their problems. An intense drought had parched the lands along Walker River. There were no grass seeds, berries, or pine nuts to be gathered. Farm tools provided by the government arrived late, and when they did come they were in short supply. Diseases raised havoc in the winter villages. In 1867 typhoid and other fevers brought swift death to nearly one hundred Trout Eaters; in 1868 measles brought death to twenty-five others, mostly children.

The mood on the reservation was somber. Death was in the air. In Mason Valley, Wodziwob (Grey Hair), a Trout Eater prophet, went into a trance. He lay deadly still. It appeared as if life had been drained from him. When he awoke he began to talk. He had visited the dead and had talked to the spirits. Soon the recently stricken would return to earth. They would bring eternal life back with them. Soon the land, now parched beyond belief and devoid of life, would team with seeds, nuts, and berries, with fish, wild flowers, and an abundant animal life. No longer would there be want, starvation, death.

Wodziwob attended the Trout Eater festivals; he preached at the circle dances. He visited with the Cuiui Eaters. And others carried his message to the Indian tribes of the western states.

The Trout Eaters held Wodziwob in high regard. They viewed him as a special shaman, one who through the powers given him by the spirits could bring back the dead and change the weather. They willingly danced the Ghost Dance with hopes high. The Cuiui Eaters, on the other hand, viewed Wodziwob quite differently. They saw him as a prophet. They were skeptical about his ability to return the dead to life. They would wait and see.

By Walker River the Trout Eaters danced in 1869, 1870, 1871, and again in 1872. But the drought remained and the dead did not return. Fortunately 1873 was a better year. The Trout Eaters gathered a bumper pine nut crop and the government furnished them with tools and wagons for work on their irrigation ditches and dams. The Ghost Dance fell into limbo.

Sixteen years later the Ghost Dance was revived when Wovoka (The Cutter), who was also from Mason Valley, had a revelation directly from God. It was God who told him to tell his people to be good, to live in peace. It was God who gave Wovoka the dance and with it control of the elements. It was God who promised that if the people danced for five consecutive days they would be rewarded with perpetual happiness, that the spirits of those long dead would be returned to earth.

On the reservation in 1890 the Trout Eaters, inspired by Wovoka, danced. And Wovoka's message – like Wodziwob's before him – was carried far and wide. It even reached the Sioux at Pine Ridge in South Dakota, where in a different setting the Indians were encouraged to prepare for war.

But the spirits of the dead did not return to Walker River in

1890, 1891, or 1892. And Wovoka – or Jack Wilson as he was called by the whites – the respected shaman of the Trout Eaters, was off in Mason Valley hunting the rabbit. The Ghost Dance would go into limbo once more.

Schools, Churches, and Doctors. Meanwhile at Pyramid Lake there were further changes. A vocational school had been opened on the reservation in 1878, a day school in 1879. The Cuiui Eaters responded slowly at first, but then eagerly. Kwina's grandchildren were three of fifty-two students in attendance. They helped to clear the brush for the school farm in the summer of 1883. Two years later they moved into the Pyramid Lake Boarding School where they were taught reading, writing, and spelling. They drew pictures and sang songs. They loved to play musical instruments, especially the organ.

On the school farm the boys raised pumpkins, squash, turnips, cabbages, carrots, melons, and onions. The girls learned to work with needle and thread. They made dresses, shirts, sheets, and aprons. They learned to cook and keep house.

In 1891 a day school was opened at Wadsworth. And some of the children were sent to the Stewart Indian School near Carson City where they attended classes with Washoes, Shoshones, and other Paiutes.

While the Cuiui Eaters were learning the white man's ways in school they were also beginning to feel the impact of the white man's churches and the white man's doctor. A Baptist missionary served as Indian agent at Wadsworth in 1875. He held his services at Nixon. The Episcopalians built churches at Wadsworth and Nixon. After the first year they could report the baptism of eight adults and thirty-two children. The Cuiui Eaters who attended services enjoyed the Episcopalian ritual. But the missionaries acknowledged that their work was difficult. They would have to "make haste slowly."

In 1886 a resident physician was stationed at Wadsworth. Rather reluctantly, perhaps, the Cuiui Eaters began to seek his help. Kwina's son went to him when his children were ill. However, when old

Kwina became ill while driving his wagon and team of horses south into Brunswick Canyon during the autumn pine nut harvest, he called upon a shaman for help. Many others, sick or dying, continued to call upon the Indian curer. The white doctors, like the white churchmen, would "make haste slowly."

An Appraisal of the American Impact

On his death bed in 1893 – and under the eyes of a shaman – Kwina could reflect upon the American impact. He remembered the quiet and wonderful life at Humboldt Sink before Joseph Walker's visit. He remembered the fight and his growing hostility toward the white man. He remembered the white-topped wagons that rolled past the tule swath and how they barred the Ground Squirrel Eaters from river and lake. He recalled the decision that he and Paxu had made – the decision to leave the sink and move to Pyramid Lake.

And as if in a dream he remembered the wars and the retreat to safety along the western side of Winnemucca Lake. He remembered the Chinese laborers and the coming of the "iron horse." He remembered the beginnings of the reservation, the coming of the entrymen, the futile attempts at farming. He remembered Wodziwob's visit, his preaching, and talk of the Ghost Dance.

When the shaman reached a high note in his song Kwina remembered Wadsworth – the railroad depot, the ramshackle karnees at the edge of the white town, the home of Abraham Newberry where his son worked hard for wages, the school where his grandchildren . . .

And in a brief moment he remembered Paxu with tumpline, burden basket, and stone knife moving gracefully between the rice grass shoots near Humboldt Lake. In another moment Kwina was dead. His ramshackle karnee at the edge of town was burned and he was laid to rest in the cemetery at Nixon.

The American impact? It was devastating! And it had all occurred in the space of one man's lifetime!

>> 5 <<

THE TWENTIETH CENTURY

In the Humboldt Valley the Ground Squirrel Eaters and Sagebrush Mountain Dwellers had flocked into the towns – Oreana, Lovelock, Mill City, Winnemucca – seeking employment. Occasionally young children, inspired by their parents, paid visits to local gravesites – like those of Kwahadu and Mua, of Huna and Pagunupa. Pagunupa's grandchildren visited quite often. One had married a white man who was employed at the new Toulon Tungsten Mill (1916) south of Lovelock. The gravesite was not far away.

On Walker River the Trout Eaters were preoccupied with the opening of their reservation to white settlers and the allotment of their lands. On May 25, 1906, the Trout Eaters ceded 268,000 acres including Walker Lake to the United States government. In return each family head was to receive a twenty-acre tract or allotment plus $300. Actually each family head got only $25 in 1906; in 1907 they were paid the remainder in goods – a wagon, a mowing machine, a plow, a harness, a stove, a saw, a hammer. And they had lost in the process most of their valuable land base.

Coyote was obviously at work! On October 29, 1906, the reservation was officially opened to white settlement. By 1908 white people were even leasing the allotted lands. They began to build various businesses, stores, corrals, and warehouses on the Indian acres. And the Trout Eaters themselves, without employment on the reservation, attempted to find jobs elsewhere.

At Pyramid Lake, near the gravesites of Kwina and Paxu, the Cuiui Eaters were experiencing even greater difficulties. The very life of the lake itself was at stake.

In 1902 Congress had passed the so-called Reclamation Act. Its chief sponsor, Francis G. Newlands of Nevada, believed that implementation of the act would help to make the Nevada desert an agricultural paradise. Waters from the Carson and Truckee rivers would be used to irrigate the land southeast of Pyramid Lake.

Accordingly Derby Dam was built across the lower Truckee (1905). And the river's waters were diverted by canal and a series of laterals into the desert. Nevada's farmers and cattle ranchers were hopeful. They beamed with optimism. But for the Cuiui Eaters the diversion of the Truckee's water was only another nightmare.

Pyramid Lake began to shrink. Sandbars appeared at the Truckee's mouth. The cutthroat trout, long a mainstay in the Cuiui diet, could no longer ascend the river to spawn. The cuiui itself was threatened but managed to reproduce near the lake's shoreline. By 1935 the last of the cutthroat trout were struggling for existence. By 1939 they had disappeared entirely.

But the lake continued to survive as the Cuiui Eaters, aroused by the actions of the federal government, began to battle back. In 1956 the Washoe Project, to build flood control dams on the upper Carson and Truckee rivers, made it mandatory that water be released to Pyramid Lake. It also called for the restoration of the fishery.

But the water was not forthcoming. A government task force report in 1964 merely suggested that ". . . every effort to maintain the greatest practicable flow of water into Pyramid Lake . . ." be encouraged.

In less than one hundred years the lake had dropped over 80 feet; between 1962 and 1966 it dropped 5 feet more. And even as recently

as 1969 there were responsible government officials who were advocating a further drop – 152 feet – that would stabilize the lake level!

On the reservation the economic situation deteriorated. In 1970 the unemployment rate stood at 70 percent. More than 50 percent of the families had annual incomes of less than $2,000. Cuiui Eaters could not survive without the aid of pensions, welfare, and general food distribution.

In the same year the Secretary of the Interior announced that the amount of water going to the Newlands Project would be reduced, thereby increasing the amount going to Pyramid Lake. Unfortunately the amount was hardly enough to maintain the lake's stability.

The case went to the courts and was tried in October, 1972, in Washington, D.C. As a result the judge ordered the Secretary of the Interior to fulfill his duty and make available all water to Pyramid Lake ". . . not obligated by court decree or contract . . ." with the District of Nevada.

It was a victory at last for Wolf, the Good Brother. Had it come in time to save the Cuiui Eaters at Pyramid Lake?

A Final Word

The Gatherers of old, who roamed the salt flats and nestled in their warm winter karnees, no longer exist. But their descendants live on. In the Nevada Indian Agency today there are no fewer than fourteen reservations and twelve so-called colonies. At Pyramid Lake there is a population of over 400; at Walker River over 450; at Lovelock, near the old haunt of the Ground Squirrel Eaters, over 100. There are Paiutes in Carson City, in Sparks, in the Reno ghetto, and elsewhere in urban America.

They can all look back with much pride to their heritage as The Gatherers. They can view themselves today with deep satisfaction as they manage their own resources, fight their own battles in the courts, and write their own history. They can look forward to a new future that they themselves can help to shape.

>> GLOSSARY <<

allotment – the division of reservation lands into small tracts as provided by the General Allotment Act (1887).

atlatl – a spear-throwing device that helped increase distance and power.

bulrush – large rush found on wet land or in water.

camelid – small North American camel of the Pleistocene.

Danger Cave – on the edge of the great Salt Desert in western Utah.

entrada – Spanish word for entrance.

entrymen – the term often applied to squatters on Paiute land.

hand game – played with small bone sticks – one marked, the other unmarked – that could be concealed in the hands.

karnee – a typically dome-shaped shelter built by the Paiute, made of light willow poles and covered with sagebrush, grass, or tule mats.

pine nut – a staple in the Paiute diet that is plucked from the branches of the one-leaf piñon tree.

rendezvous – summer meeting place of the American fur trappers and those who supplied them with goods from the east.

shaman – medicine man.

shinny – a game much like hockey, the object of which was to drive a puck made of braided cloth over the opposing team's goal.

sweat lodge – extra large karnee that was used as the meeting place of men and young boys.

tule – a variety of bulrush found in the marshy areas of the Great Basin.

>> BIBLIOGRAPHY <<

Cline, Gloria G. *Exploring the Great Basin.* Norman: University of Oklahoma Press, 1963.

——. *Peter Skene Ogden and the Hudson's Bay Company.* Norman: University of Oklahoma Press, 1974.

Costello, David F. *The Desert World.* New York: Thomas Y. Crowell Company, 1972.

d'Azevedo, Warren L. et al., eds. *The Current Status of Anthropological Research in the Great Basin: 1964.* Reno: Desert Research Institute, 1966.

Dorn, Edward. *The Shoshoneans.* New York: William Morrow and Company, Inc., 1966.

Elliott, Russell R. *History of Nevada.* Lincoln: University of Nebraska Press, 1973.

Ewers, John C., ed. *Adventures of Zenas Leonard, Fur Trader.* Norman: University of Oklahoma Press, 1959.

Facts about Nevada Agency. United States Department of the Interior. Stewart, Nev.: Bureau of Indian Affairs, January 1974.

Goodwin, Victor O. *The Humboldt – Nevada's Desert River and Thoroughfare of the American West.* U.S.D.A. – Nevada Humboldt River Basin Survey, 1966.

Harnar, Nellie S. *The History of the Pyramid Lake Indians, 1843–1959, and Early Tribal History, 1825–1834.* Sparks, Nev.: Dave's Printing and Publishing, 1974.

Heizer, Robert F., and Kreiger, Alex D. "The Archaeology of Humboldt Cave, Churchill County, Nevada," *University of California Publications in American Archaeology and Ethnology*, vol. 47, 1956, pp. 1–190.

Hermann, Ruth. *The Paiutes of Pyramid Lake.* San Jose: Harlan-Young Press, 1972.

Irving, Washington, ed. *The Adventures of Captain Bonneville, U.S.A.* Norman: University of Oklahoma Press, 1961.

Jackson, Donald, and Spence, Mary Lee. eds. *The Expeditions of John Charles Fremont.* vol. 1. Urbana: University of Illinois Press, 1970.

Jaeger, Edmund C. *The North American Deserts.* Stanford: Stanford University Press, 1957.

Jennings, Jesse D. *Prehistory of North America.* 2d ed. New York: McGraw-Hill, 1974.

Johnson, Edward C. *Walker River Paiutes: A Tribal History.* Schurz, Nev.: Walker River Paiute Tribe, 1975.

Kraus, George. *High Road to Promontory.* New York: Castle Books, 1969.

Loud, Llewellyn L., and Harrington, M. R. "Lovelock Cave," *University of California Publications in American Archaeology and Ethnology*, vol. XXV, 1929, pp. vii–183.

Morgan, Dale L. *The Humboldt, Highroad of the West.* New York and Toronto: Farrar and Rinehart, 1943.

——. *Jedidiah Smith and the Opening of the West.* Indianapolis: Bobbs-Merrill Co., 1953.

Nevins, Allan. *Fremont, Pathmarker of the West.* New York: Longman's Green, 1955.

Paul, Rodman W. *Mining Frontiers of the Far West, 1848–1880.* New York: Holt, Rinehart and Winston, 1963.

Scott, Lalla. *Karnee.* Reno: University of Nevada Press, 1966.

Steward, Julian H. *Basin-Plateau Aboriginal Sociopolitical Groups.* Bureau of American Ethnology, Bulletin 120, Washington, 1938.

——. "Ethnography of the Owens Valley Paiute," *University of California Publications in American Archaeology and Ethnology*, vol. XXXIII, 1932–1934, pp. 233–350.

Stewart, Julian H., and Wheeler-Voegelin, Erminie. *Paiute Indians III.* New York and London: Garland Publishing, Inc., 1974.

Stewart, George R., ed. *The Opening of the California Trail.* Berkeley and Los Angeles: University of California Press, 1953.

——. *The California Trail.* New York: McGraw-Hill, 1962.

The War of Ghosts, 1902–1972, *Announcements*, The National Indian Law Library, November–December, 1972.

Wheat, Margaret M. *Survival Arts of the Primitive Paiutes.* Reno: University of Nevada Press, 1967.

Wheeler, Sessions S. *The Desert Lake: The Story of Nevada's Pyramid Lake.* Caldwell, Idaho: The Caxton Printers, Ltd., 1967.

Willey, Gordon R. *An Introduction to American Archaeology.* vol. 1, North and Middle America. Englewood Cliffs, N. J.: Prentice-Hall, 1966.

Wright, William. *History of the Big Bonanza.* Hartford: American Publishing Company, 1876.

>> SELECTED READING << FOR YOUNG PEOPLE

Baldwin, Gordon C. *How Indians Really Lived.* New York: G. P. Putnam's Sons, 1967.

Bauer, Helen. *California Indian Days.* Garden City, N. Y.: Doubleday and Company, Inc., 1968.

Berry, Don. *Mountain Men: The Trappers of the Great Fur Trading Era.* New York: Macmillan, 1966.

Billard, Jules B., ed. *The World of the American Indian.* Washington, D.C.: National Geographic Society, 1974.

Brandon, William. *American Heritage Book of Indians.* New York: Dell Publishing Company, Inc., 1961.

Burt, O. W. *Jedidiah Smith, Fur Trapper of the Old West.* New York: Julian Messner, 1951.

Haines, Francis. *Indians of the Great Basin and Plateau.* New York: G. P. Putnam's Sons, 1970.

Hoyt, Olga. *American Indians Today.* New York and London: Abelard-Schuman, 1972.

Jacobson, Daniel. *The First Americans*. Boston: Ginn and Company, 1969.

——. *Great Indian Tribes*. Maplewood, N. J.: Hammond, Inc., 1970.

Josephy, Jr., Alvin M. *The Indian Heritage of America*. New York: Bantam Books, Inc., 1969.

Lavine, Sigmund A. *The Games the Indians Played*. New York: Dodd, Mead and Company, 1974.

McNeer, May, and Ward, Lynd. *The American Indian Story*. New York: Ariel Books, 1963.

Tunis, Edwin. *Indians*. Cleveland and New York: The World Publishing Company, 1959.

Vlahos, Olivia. *New World Beginnings; Indian Cultures in the Americas*. New York: Viking, 1970.

>> INDEX <<

>> ABOUT THE AUTHOR <<

Daniel Jacobson is the director of the Social Science Teaching Institute, professor of geography and education, and adjunct professor of anthropology at Michigan State University. He has been deeply involved in the history, culture, and present-day situation of the American Indian. Dr. Jacobson is the author of *Great Indian Tribes* and *The First Americans.* He is also a contributor to *The Book of Knowledge* and has written many articles on the culture of North American Indians. *The Hunters* and *The Fishermen* are other books in this Indians of North America series.

>> ABOUT THE ARTIST <<

Since his graduation from Pratt Institute, Richard Cuffari has illustrated over eighty books, winning praises from the American Institute of Graphic Arts, the Society of Illustrators, the Christopher Award, and the Children's Book Council Showcase Exhibit. Mr. Cuffari was born and educated in Brooklyn and continues to make his home there. He is illustrating all of Daniel Jacobson's books in the Indians of North America series.